W9-AEX-491

Surfaces in Creative Drawing

Ernst Röttger, Dieter Klante, and Friedrich Salzmann

Surfaces in Creative Drawing

Van Nostrand Reinhold Company, New York

745
R74s
82895
apr. 1973

© Otto Maier Verlag, Ravensburg, Germany, 1969

Published in the United States of America 1970
by Van Nostrand Reinhold Company
450 West 33 Street, New York, N.Y. 10001
Library of Congress Catalog Card Number 75-119597

Printed in Holland

Contents

Introduction

In this volume we aim to reveal the part which can be played by surfaces in creative design. By means of separate examples and exercises we shall become familiar with the possibilities this medium offers for self-expression; and we shall develop a course designed to stimulate creative powers, imagination and invention. We address ourselves to all those who enjoy creating objects in tangible form; teachers especially can profit from this book.

Amongst those elements which go to make a picture, the surface assumes a special importance. The idea 'surface' has here a double significance. Just like a point, a line or a dab of colour, so a 'surface' as a grey or black area is a means of creative expression, for it is associated with the forming of shapes. At the same time, however, the 'surface' is the background and basis of all pictorial composition in every range of drawing and painting, and even further in the spheres of the plastic arts and architecture.

There is no end to the range of shapes that can be created by playing with the surface. The present volume can accordingly offer only modest stimuli, hints for layman and teacher alike on how to gain an understanding of the part played by the surface in creating shapes. We shall not deal with any expensive processes. We have rather taken pains to develop elementary games sequences which, for all their simplicity, are suitable as technical processes to make us aware of their rich variety of forms, and their relationship with one another.

This volume offers examples of the lay-out of the surface itself, the arrangement of dots as surface shapes or as organic or geometric patterns; these begin against a background of contrasting black and white and reach sensitive tones of grey and pattern formations, whose surprisingly close relationship to the compositions and shapes in nature is shown in a series of examples. This is particularly true of the sequence of games which deal with creating shapes with spots, or by taking prints and impressions, or by folding and pressing. These series are developed naturally and seem to us admirably suited to draw attention to the close relationship which exists between the rules of pictorial composition and those of the world of nature.

In the text of the individual chapters the creative processes and methods of shape-making are for the most part dealt with formally. Some general considerations, valid for every type of work, should therefore be made concerning the nature of this play method and the way exercises are set. Our play method does not approach a creative exercise with a firm conception of the picture already in mind, nor with the creative materials already predetermined by some pictorial image. Our method springs from these very media themselves, seeking such possibilities of self-expression as are suitable to each. This game is not directed to a certain objective, and remains undetermined as to its results; but it thereby ensures that complete freedom of action which is not hampered by the necessity of having to reach a set target. Discoveries are made during the game. We are prepared for surprises and profit from the gifts of chance. The products of experience and of accident are evaluated, taken over, and consciously applied. The method inspires the exploration of new paths. In this play method, what one learns from one's work is more highly esteemed than the visible result.

To be meaningful, a game must have rules. This game with creative media is accordingly so guided by rules that a disciplined analysis is possible, with freedom and restraint in proper proportions. And thus we can also learn that plastic creation—in Gropius' perceptive definition—is not mere arbitrary caprice, but is based on freedom of action within strictly regulated limits.

The rules of the game must be unambiguous; they determine the area of manoeuvre whose limits are binding on everyone. They must give separate instructions concerning the materials, tools, methods and types of pictures and shapes to be used, and their arrangement.

This volume, like the others in the series, has also been conceived completely pictorially; it is primarily from the pictures that information and stimuli will emerge. The verbal text is limited to only the barest explanations.

The illustrations show the results of games and exercises in creative modelling which were carried out by children, young people, adults, laymen and students. We have chosen them for their formal quality, and they are meant to be nothing more than examples. Mere imitation we cannot prevent; but it is precisely here that the danger of degeneration lies, degeneration into mere formalism, into the cliché. The principle of learning by playing with creative materials excludes mere mechanical appropriation of an idea by either anticipation or imitation. The principle rather liberates those creative powers which condition one's individual achievement and the revelation and discovery of oneself; it is to be understood in this sense alone.

Symbols used:

S = Work of students of the State High School of Applied Arts in Kassel and Hamburg, and of the Teachers'
Technical Institute, Kassel

T = Work from teachers' training courses

B = Work by boys

G = Work by girls

The subsequent figures show the pupils' ages.

Designing with Dots

The dot or spot has a special relationship with the surface; when we separate the surface forms into the two main groups, organic and geometric, we include it in the former. We find the dot everywhere in nature: in a landscape, in the worlds of plants and animals, in geology. We find it in drawings of flowers and leaves, in the camouflage of insects and wild cats, in markings on stones and land formations. And when we use the microscope it surprises us by the extent of its variety and richness.

As in nature, so also in our play method: the variety of spotted surface shapes is caused by allowing a dye to drip on to the surface, or by pressing or pulling out a piece from the dyed material, or by wiping, spraying or dabbing it. Its shape and character are largely conditioned by the method used in making it.

Illustrations 1-6 show some examples of both firmly outlined and also gently spreading shapes made from spots.

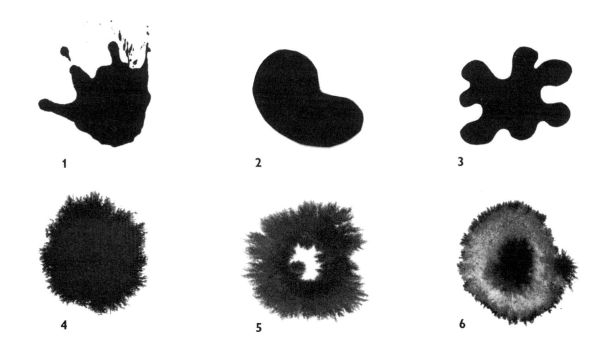

1: A blot. A firm shape in a set direction made by allowing drops to fall diagonally.

2: A firmly outlined spot painted with brush and indian ink.

3: A curved organic shape painted with brush and indian ink.

4: A spot dripped on to a damp paper surface. The dye runs and gives a gently spreading outline.

5: A spot within a spot. The centre is emphasized by leaving a blank area inside. The indian ink spreads freely on well-soaked paper.

6: A picturesque spot, producing a quite plastic and stereoscopic effect. Several coats of indian ink, thinned down as required, on damp paper.

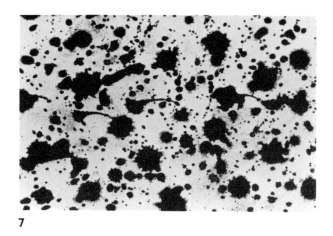

7

8

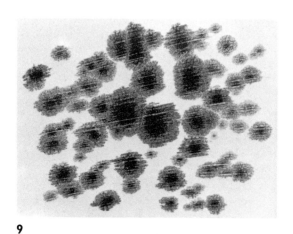

9

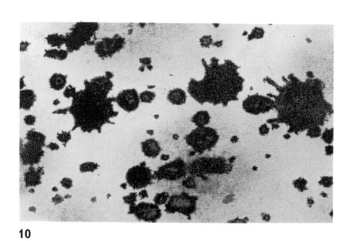

10

7: Indian ink dripped and sprayed from various heights on to drawing paper.

8: A paint wash on Ingres paper. The spots are made with a paint brush on damp paper and spread gently over the surface (so-called wet-on-wet process).

9: Poster paint dripped from the paint brush on cartridge paper with cellulose coating.

10: A slightly cloudy background surface is prepared by the wet-on-wet method; when this is dry, various-sized blots of indian ink are dripped on, giving firm outlines.

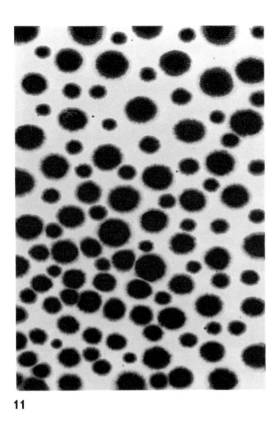

11

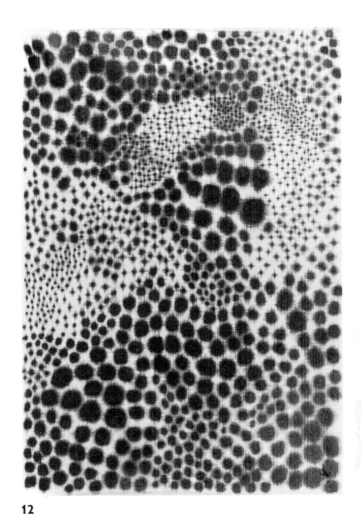

12

11: On a sheet of blotting paper the paint drops lose their colour, though the rings remain clear, like water drops.

12: Paint drops on woven material, in this case thin linen, assume very clearly the shape of the weave.

The examples so far have shown the spot in various shapes caused by different materials and methods; it is already becoming clear that there must be a period of free experiment before further constructive materials are introduced; this will be a preliminary to the closely regulated formative tasks which follow.

For the simpler processes, like cutting along folds or wiping, this free-play period should be short. But for methods which show a greater range of variation in both technical media and practical handling, this period preceding the creative process must be longer and more intensive; its results are likely to be affected to a greater extent by chance, and the process must even be interrupted now and again. The aim of this period is to test, to seek and to find. The free game becomes an experiment in which given technical situations are explored, and formal possibilities are discovered at the same time.

Once the requisite basic experience has been gained, the actual modelling tasks must be limited according to the student's capacity. Experience teaches us that, especially in the early exercises, strict limitation is of the greatest assistance. As examples of such strictly limited tasks let us mention simple stampings (p. 44); here only one way of making a shape was being used, and the surface build-up was carried out in strict sequence. Even in exercises in the objective and figurative range, where a clear aim is already in mind, the technical means and formative materials should be exactly prescribed beforehand, at least to begin with.

The spot game begins quite freely, in the full sense of the word, and is aimed at exploring by experiment the possibilities offered by various kinds of paper and coloured liquids. (Experiments with smooth and rough surface backgrounds, and those which absorb or reject water: drawing paper, writing paper, Ingres paper, tinted paper, wrapping paper, tissue paper, wallpaper; preparation of the undersurface: damping, covering with glue, crumpling etc.; the use then of soluble paint in various thicknesses: ink, indian ink, water colours and coloured washes, poster paints, etc.)

13-21: Cut-outs from a systematic series of exercises which break up a surface and use spots to form various shades of grey. Related compositions appear in both the vertical and horizontal lines of pictures. Arranged vertically, the exercises illustrate, in the left-hand row, the shading off of a surface from black to white by a gentle recession of the former colour; in the middle panel this is achieved according to the principle of movement to the centre, and on the right by movement either to or from the centre of the sheet.

Similar techniques are occasionally used in the horizontal arrangement. 13-15 show the dabbing technique,

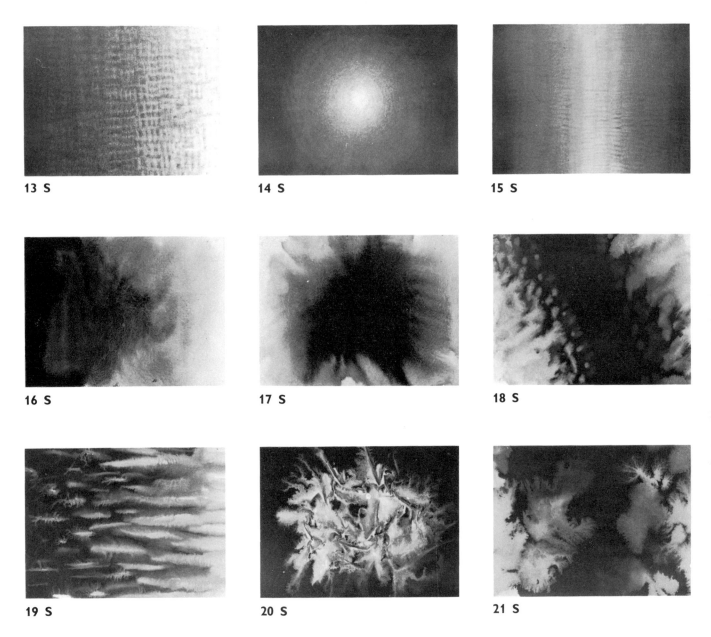

13 S 14 S 15 S

16 S 17 S 18 S

19 S 20 S 21 S

white poster paint dabbed on black cartridge paper with a bristle brush; 16-18 the wet-on-wet method with a paint wash; 19-21 the wet-on-wet method with dyes—here a successful result was achieved by applying the paint while the wash was still drying.

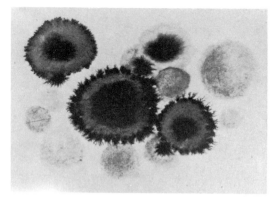

22 S

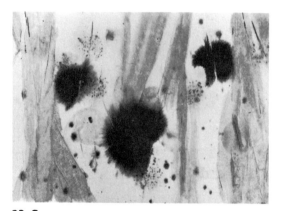

23 S

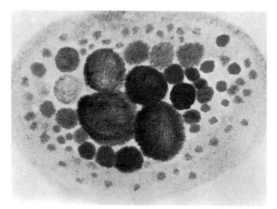

24 S

Examples of intentional pattern-making with spots using various processes.

22-24: The surface is treated by the wet-on-wet process, so that the painted spot can be developed outwards. Arranged with a view to making contrasts in a loose scatter. A transparent paint is applied with various dye materials so that the background colour shows through on to Ingres paper (8×12 inches) and smooth cartridge paper (12×16 inches).

25: Wet-on-wet method; indian ink on cartridge paper (12×16 inches).

26: A technically complicated method in which soluble paint and oil paint were applied together. The colours reject one another. While the picture is being constructed, the surface lay-out is strongly affected by the materials used. The white dots are produced by covering an area with drops from a wax candle, which prevents the paint from spreading on to the undersurface.

25 S

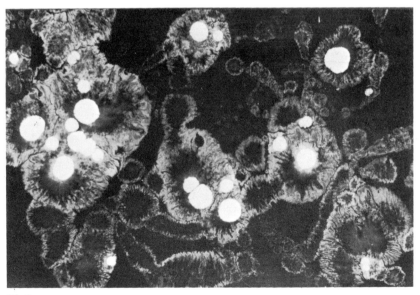

26 S

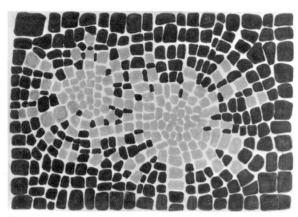

27 S

28 S

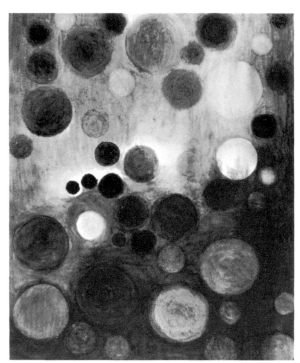

29 S

27: Centred along two axes by building up with grey and black spots; painted with thick felt pencils. 12 × 16 inches.

28: The surface is broken up with the help of torn-off pieces of paper used as templates or transfers. Paint is dabbed on to the moist surface below. 12 × 16 inches.

29: Circular shapes of various sizes scattered to form patterns. The paint has been applied by the wet-on-wet method and dabbed on additionally in places with absorbent paper (blotting paper or a paper tissue). 12 × 16 inches.

Plate 1: Surface treated with drops of paint using the wet-on-wet method.

G 15

35   36   37

Prints

Paint is dripped on to a glass plate or other hard background, and then pressed away with a piece of paper. When this paper is lifted off, the particles of paint have arranged themselves in charming shapes, both gently spreading and also firmly outlined, and with most delicate designs inside. There appear shapes from the vegetable world, fantastic growths such as lichens, mosses, corals, leaves and flowers; structures emerge reminding us of stonelike shapes (tufa: 38, 39), or rotten wood (41). And great savage landscapes torn by ravines are disclosed.

This is a game where chance plays, too, and has fresh surprises always at hand. This is an extremely fertile situation for a constructive game, for what appears to be chance can to quite a large extent be directed in one's own experiments.

The microscopic shapes illustrated here in almost natural size are produced by a paint wash, thin indian ink, and poster paint. The paper must be well-glazed if water paints are to be wiped off; slightly glued absorbent papers are suitable under only certain conditions, but may be used with paints made from paste. The types of pattern created depend largely on the method used when withdrawing the paper, as well as on the dye used.

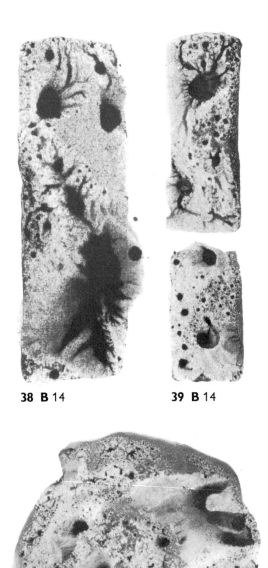

38 B 14　　　　**39 B** 14

40 T

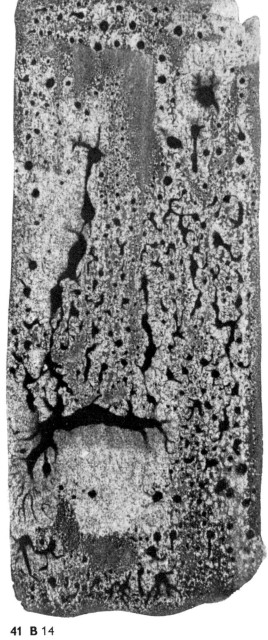

41 B 14

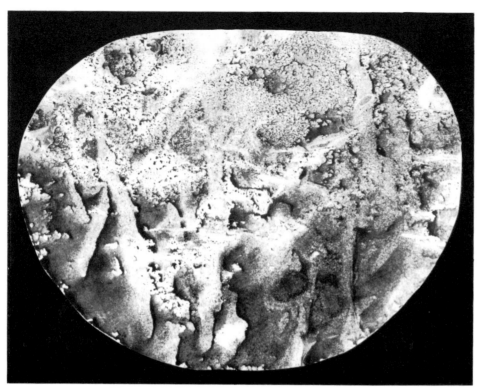

42 T

Firm pressure gives a delicate drawing, whereas the paint remains loosely on the surface if it is loosely applied. But everyone must try this for himself.

The spot that has been cleared does not need to be left wholly exposed.

In 40 there emerged from the 'accidental' rock-like structure the additional shape of a stone that could be cut out.

In 42 we tried to make from a rather large print a suitable cut-out with a holed stencil; it was later covered over with black passepartout.

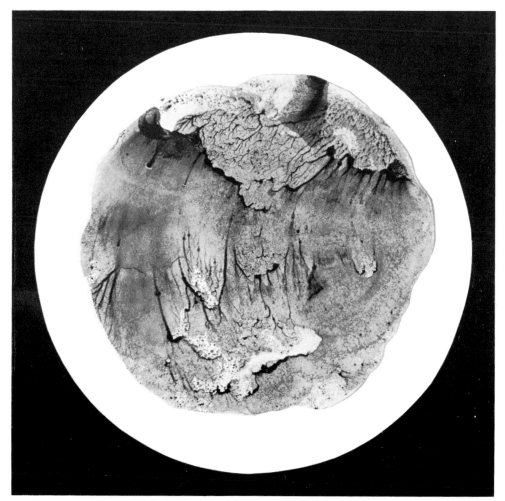

43 T

In 43 the shape has been cut out with scissors, and with a sensitive feeling for the tender bud-like fruit shape.

23

44 T

The surface has here been treated from the first with a definite aim in mind.

44: A paint wash was applied to thick drawing paper with large and small drops in horizontal rows; this paper was then covered with a second sheet, and by passing the lino roller across it strips of various width were rolled out horizontally.

45: Print taken from a glass plate stained with thin lacquer. The resulting impression is not wholly a chance product, but the result of a directed procedure (agreed quantity of paint applied, pressure partly with finger tips and ball of the thumb, rolling and withdrawal in definite directions). Similar treatment can produce similar effects at will, even if not the same shapes.

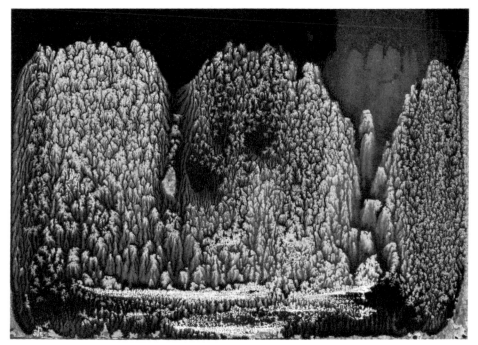

45 T

After the paper has been withdrawn the negative remains on the glass plate, and in the change over from black to white this occasionally makes the negative even more effective than the positive. So long as the paint remains damp a second print may be taken; it is most successful on smooth, rather damp paper. When doing this the plate must be carefully rubbed, so that the paper takes up as much as possible of the relatively small amount of paint. The positive shown on pages 26, 27 was made from such a previously prepared glass plate, and the second print was taken by this method. The process is simple. A glass plate which has had paint rolled on to it is covered with paper shapes. When these are removed, lighter surfaces remain on the glass plate. A print can then be taken.

46 B 14

47 B 14

48 S

49 S

In 46-52 the small pieces of paper and cartridge paper are first stuck down on a cardboard surface, sometimes in several layers and overlapping one another (47, 51), so that a shallow relief is formed. An imprint of this 'relief' is then made on to the glass plate. The small pieces of paper on the plate absorb the paint, but it remains at the edges and in the gaps. If the glass plate is held up to the light the expected transfer can at once be clearly recognised and assessed. The print's character is strongly influenced by the material used for the transfer (paper, cardboard, cartridge paper) and by the kind of paint. One must try different methods. For taking prints

50 S

51 S

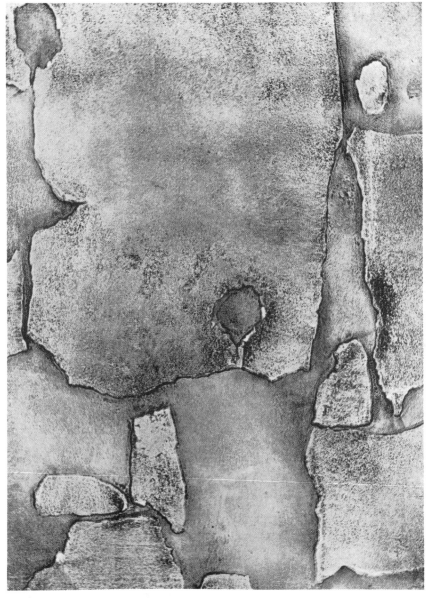

52 S

from the glass plate we recommend using paints soluble in water; these are more easily wiped off the glass plate, which has to be cleaned afresh for each print.

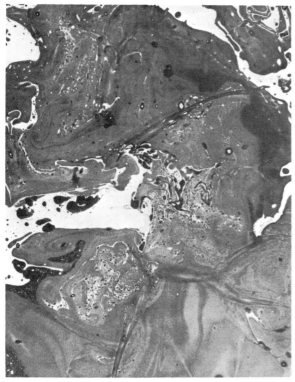

53 S

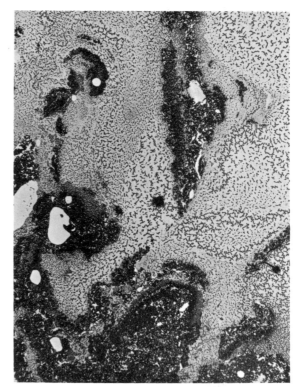

54 S

We now present five illustrated examples of a highly intractable method of taking prints, which constantly surprises us with its completely original results. The illustrations show so-called oil or turpentine papers. The method depends on the fact that oil paint is rejected by water. You require a large bowl —a rectangular photographic developing tank is best—oil paint, turpentine and paper.

Thin layers of paint containing oil or turpentine, or bound in artificial resin, are placed on a still water surface. The paint remains set in drops and spots. If a sheet of paper is laid carefully on to this prepared surface it absorbs the paint, the paint layer being lifted off as the paper is withdrawn from the surface of the water.

Plate II: Coloured 'oil paper'. Additional yellow, green and blue paint spots are dripped and painted on to the red tinted background made by the printing process described.

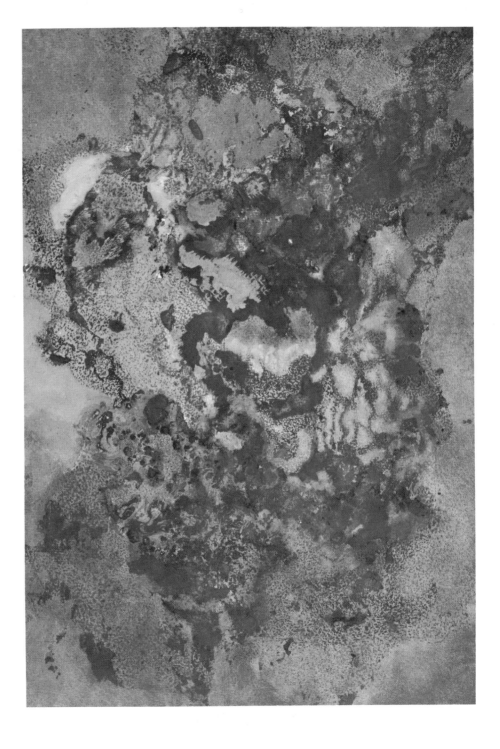

S

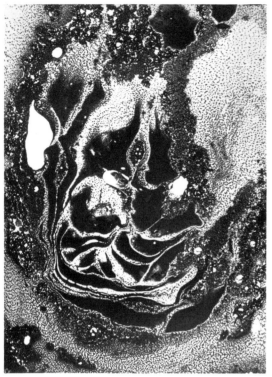

55 S

56 S

It is possible to regulate the process to a certain extent by the type of paint used, the method of applying it (pouring, dripping, spraying), the quality of the paper, and the way the paper is withdrawn. A drop of dilute detergent stirs the paint into lively motion, so that it runs into streaks. On a layer of thin cellulose the paint remains inactive, so that it can be pulled into definite shapes with a rod. This method, however, will not yield the results intended until experience has been gained by frequent experiment.

57

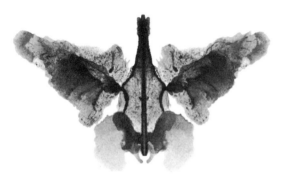

58 **G** 9

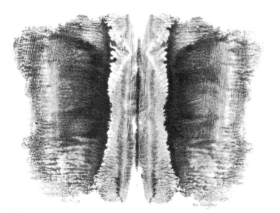

59 **B** 14

Folding and Pressing

A print made by folding is merely a special kind of print resulting naturally from the press-away-then-pull-apart technique. It actually differs from a simple print because the resulting shapes are symmetrical, as though reflected in a mirror, and this effect is most creatively significant. Even complicated images retain in their reflection a certain inner compactness.

The simplest process is drawing with blots, which children so love to do. We all know that exciting experience of our childhood days when ink blots, scattered at random on paper, transformed themselves into wondrous figures, strange beasts, ghostly shapes and fabulous creatures; one can imagine so much in them, and they challenge us to complete them with pen and brush.

This spontaneous child's game directs the teacher to a most rich creative field, which has so far been little heeded; this is no doubt because in this method chance plays a large part; it brings rich rewards, but seems not to permit the creation of planned shapes.

In the following chapter we intend to show a further development of making prints by folding; it leads us away from mere accident, and opens up new creative possibilities. We begin with a simple example of a folded print, still wholly subject to chance. But it soon becomes apparent from examples 57-61 how the technical means, the chosen colours and the backgrounds determine the print's character.

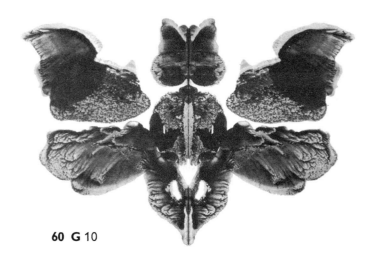

60 G 10

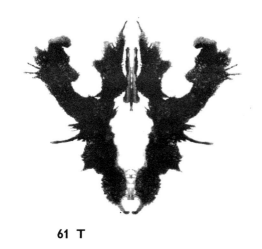

61 T

62 T

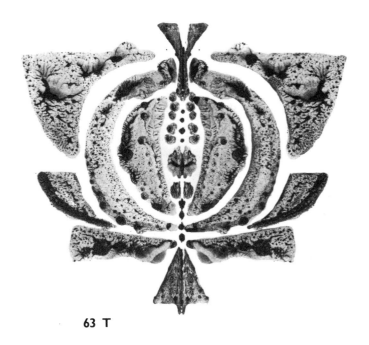

63 T

64 G 9

65 G 9

66 G 9

The two separate shapes (57) were created by pressing off the thin poster paint which had been thinly applied to a folded sheet of drawing paper; the 'Ink Butterfly' (58) was on a smooth-surfaced paper. For the more firmly outlined shape (59) the thin poster paint was pressed off from a paste-covered background; when the two sides that were sticking together were pulled apart, the paint maintained a definite line of flow along the flattened fold and in the dark areas. The 'Ink Crab' (61) emerged on a very absorbent paper, so that there is almost no internal design at all; but in 60 thin lacquer on smooth cartridge paper produced a very rich and detailed internal design.

62 and 63 are examples of guided folded prints. In 62 drops of ink on writing paper are squeezed away by vigorous pressure with the ball of the thumb and purposely arranged in order of size in an elongated oval shape. In 63 the separate shapes were painted with the brush on a half-sheet of paper and then pressed off one after the other.

Both examples show that a certain conscious shaping is possible in the folded print, both different surface lay-outs using various shape-making elements, and also designs of an almost visual objectivity.

64-66: Folded prints in original size; charming, harmoniously balanced shapes with a delicate rhythm in line and surface, with a hint of the symbolic (owl, butterfly, insect; 65 is a delicately drawn tiger's head).

67: Cut-out from a larger folded print, $\frac{3}{4}$ original size.

67 **B** 14

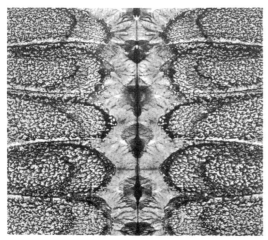

68 G 9

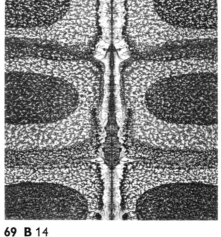

69 B 14

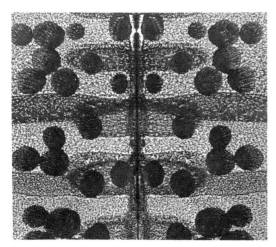

70 G 15

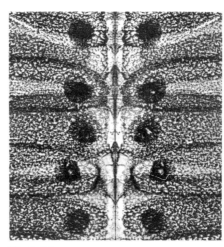

71 B 14

68-72: These show to what extent the folded print can be directed. In all these examples the surface lay-out has been achieved by the addition of an extra process. Drops of paint of uniform size dripped into or beside the fold were pressed out one after the other, being carefully rolled out in a set direction with the lino roller, so

34

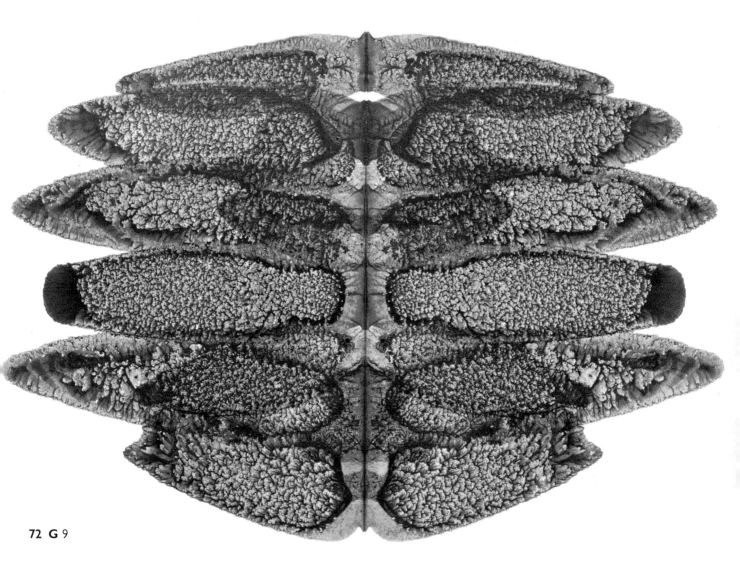

72 **G** 9

that almost similar shapes resulted. The dark patches in 69 as well as the round shapes in 70 and 71 appeared when paint was dripped on and then loosened up by pressure in going over the work a second time. All the examples were made on cartridge paper with thin lacquer.

35

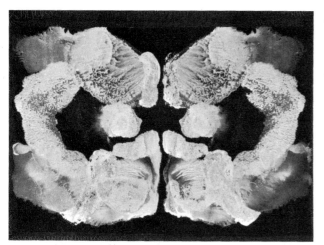

73 B 11

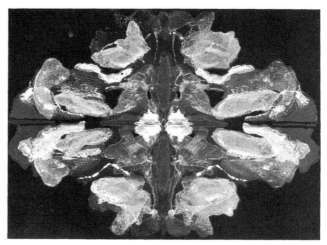

74 B 11

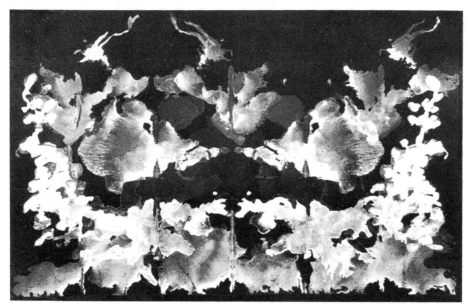

75 S

On a dark background (wrapping paper, tinted paper or photographic contact paper) it is possible to produce a folded print with layered paints. When paste paints are applied they project to a certain extent from the paper surface, as though in relief, and cause quite different shapes from those produced when the impression is made with thin paints and indian ink on white paper.

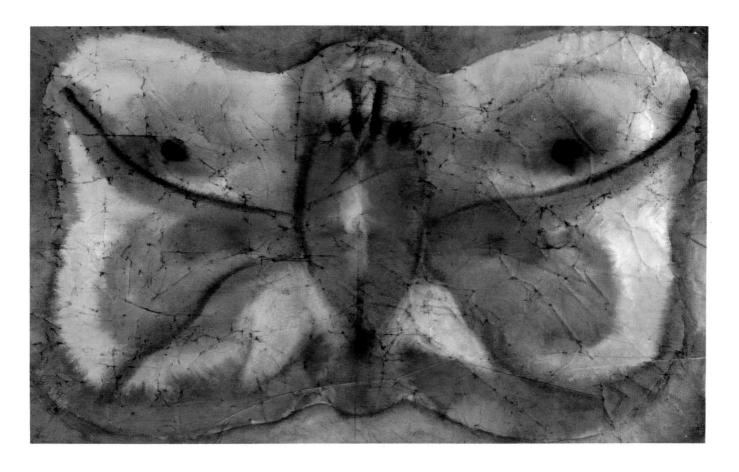

Plate III, B12: 'Butterfly'. A folded print produced by applying transparent water colours on Ingres paper; the background had been prepared by damping and crumpling.

Especially delicate colour gradations appear when bright coloured paint is used on a black background.

73: Folded print, folded once. White poster paint on photographic contact paper.

74: Folded print with double folding, horizontal and vertical, giving double symmetrical shapes. Paste paint, off-printed several times. 15 x 20 inches.

75: Folded print, five vertical folds. White poster paint on black Ingres paper. 14 x 21 inches.

76 B 10

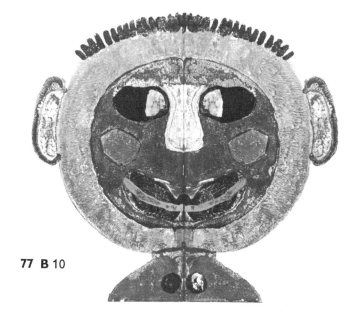

77 B 10

76: Mask, paint wash on drawing paper. 12×16 inches. Folded print only partially directed, with chance still taking a large part.

77: Head, colour wash on drawing paper. A directed folded print. In this case the shapes were painted on each side in turn; to avoid uneven distribution of the paint it was applied alternately on each side, and the impressions then taken.

78-81: Blossom, fruit, a plant and a leaf. Folded prints undertaken with an additional process in mind. In 79 and 80 we have firmly directed brushwork when painting the separate shapes. All examples with a paint wash on smooth paper.

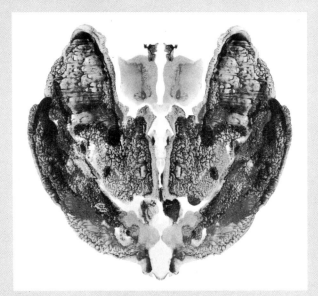

78 S

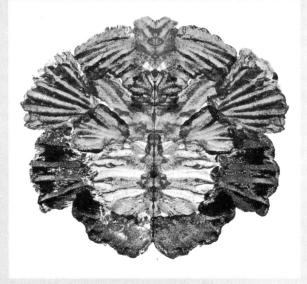

79 S

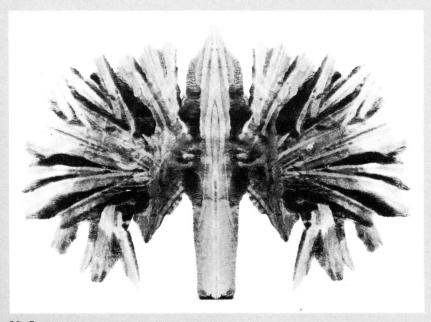

80 S

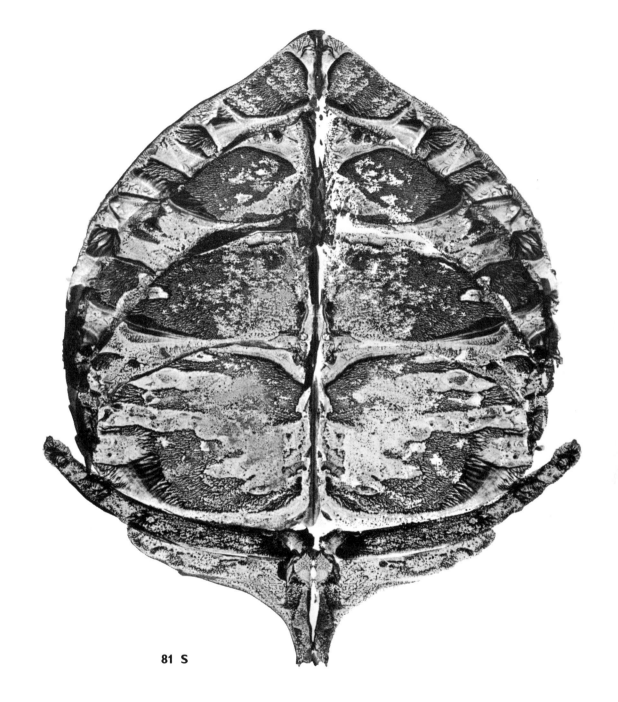

81 S

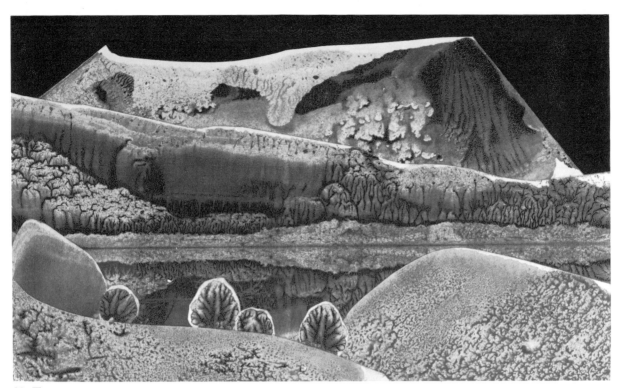

82 T

We close this chapter with some examples of folded prints and transfers suitable for montages. Shapes recalling symbolic associations are created accidentally on folded prints, and these have always stirred us to complete, interpret and emphasize the vision. Thus even blot drawings by children and imaginative adults have always been further developed by painting or drawing. But the possibility of cutting out shapes and putting them together to create new forms is, on the other hand, little used. A full and rich store of accidentally produced shapes and patterns is ready for that very purpose. We cannot of course realise in detail a picture

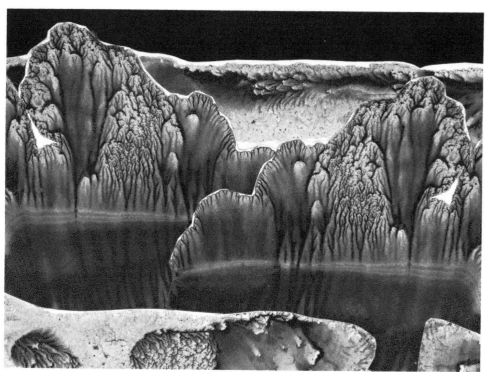

83 T

which had been previously planned and imagined. The shaping of a picture is not progressively creative but relies on seeing, recognising, choosing and piecing together whatever is to hand at the moment.

Pictorial compositions such as these landscapes have a half realistic, almost surrealistic character, which corresponds to the nature of the folds and impressions. The central area of both landscapes is from a folded print, and was mounted together with prints of various different patterns; in 83 the mirror-like reflections were rearranged.

84 **B** 14

85 **B** 14

Fabulous creatures. Montages made of sections from cut-out folded prints.

86 **B** 15

87 **B** 10

88 **B** 10

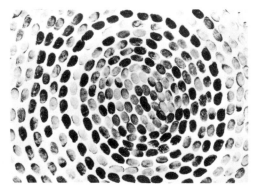

89 **B** 9

Breaking up the Surface in Shades of Grey: Stamping

Among those printing techniques which can be carried out at slight expense, the stamped or pressure print counts as a high-pressure process. The stamped print shown here aims beyond the usual idea of mere ornamental arrangements in rows and groups, or making decorative patterns on a surface. Our task here is to furnish stimuli which will produce prints whose richness lies in subtle gradations and delicate differences of colour, together with complete simplicity of form.

For so sensitive a print the technical means are important —the stamps chosen, background surfaces, colours and handling. We must experiment freely beforehand, and gain the information which is to be consciously applied later. We shall not be satisfied with the well-tried potato stamp, but shall also include for cutting stamps other materials like wood, cork, paste board, linoleum, and the newest foam materials; and we shall carry through a series of experiments with various materials and dye stuffs just as we did when playing with dots.

On the other hand we do intentionally limit ourselves to simple geometric shapes, and are sparing of incising patterns. Complicated stamped shapes are in any case not very rewarding. Only simple shapes can be added and blended to form original planned designs, and be so arranged that even untouched surfaces play their part as negative shapes.

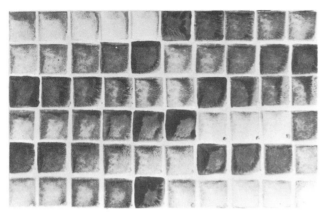

90 G 14

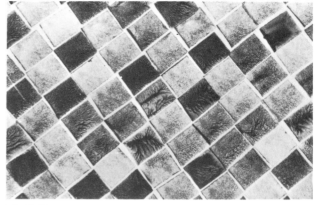

91 B 14

92 B 12

93 S

87-89: The simplest stamped print is that made by pressure with the fingers. The paint is taken up directly on the finger from the wetted palette and pressed on to the surface of the paper. When several prints are taken from one paint-covered stamp, the stamped surface grows lighter and the shades of grey fainter. The impressions remain equally clear if the stamp is covered afresh with paint after each print.

94 S

95 **B** 12

96 **B** 12

With a rectangular stamp, patterns are built up on the principle of arrangement in rows.

90, 91: Potato prints, with a paint wash on smooth cartridge paper. 8x12 inches.

92: A stamp cut from foam plastic. Colour wash on drawing paper. 8x12 inches.

93: Pattern stamped with the front face of a strip of wood beading. Print stain on Ingres paper.

94: Potato print. Poster paint on wallpaper. 12x16 inches.

95, 96: Object studies, made with four different-shaped stamps. Potato stamp with colour wash.

46

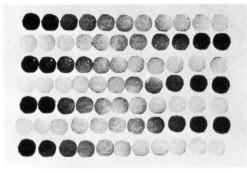

97 T

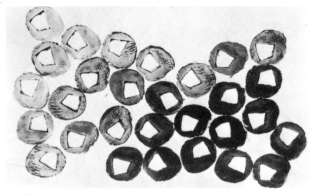

98 S

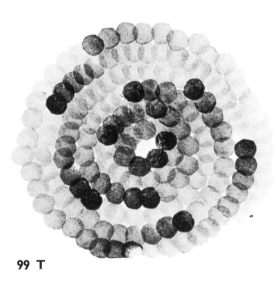

99 T

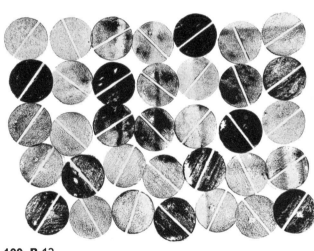

100 B 12

97, 99: Strict alignment with movement and counter-movement; lay-out built up in a spiral from the centre outwards. India rubber on a dyed ink pad. 6x8 inches.

98: Scatter. A halved potato with a rectangular shape cut out from it was used for a stamp. Adhesive paint on wallpaper. 20x12 inches.

100: Printed with a large cork grooved across the centre. Lacquer on cartridge paper. 14x10 inches.

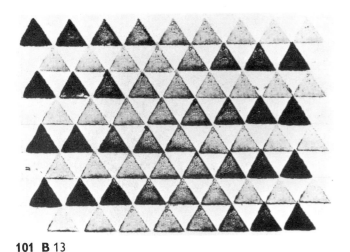

101 B 13

102 B 13

103 S

104 S

Patterns made using the triangle for shaping.

101, 102: The same shape used in strict alignment, with similar negative shapes introduced into the pattern.

Printed with a foam-plastic stamp and lacquer on Ingres paper. 12x16 inches.

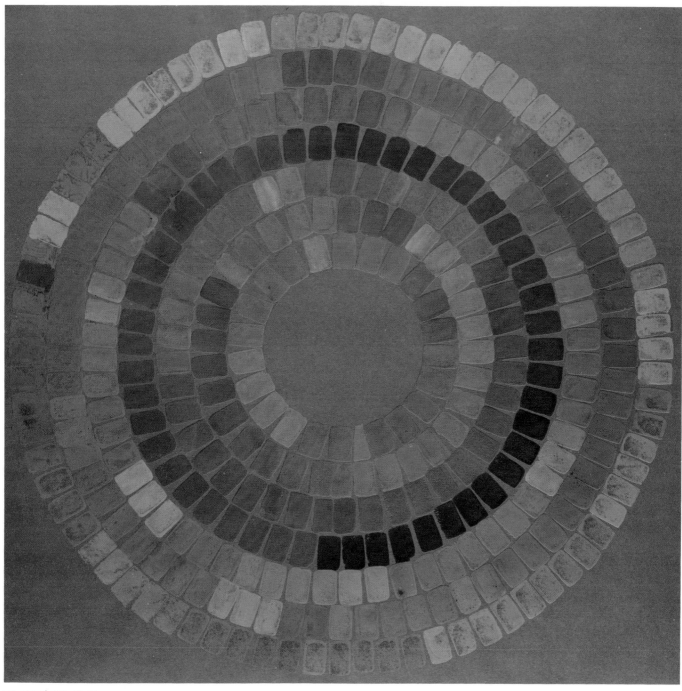

PLATE IV, B 11

105 S

103: Triangular stamp sawn out of plywood. Coloured print on cartridge paper.

104: Lay-out without blank spaces, made with two triangular stamps of related shape but different size. Stamps cut from strong pasteboard are soaked in paint and hammered on to the surface. Lacquer on tissue paper. 14x16 inches.

105: Potato print with poster paint of various thinness, on black cartridge paper. 24x11 inches.

106: Background printed beforehand with a piece of coarse linen; circular shapes impressed with the end of a round stick. Print stain on drawing paper. 12x16 inches.

107: Printed with a triangular linoleum stamp, and a cork. Lacquer. 12x16 inches.

Plate IV: Colour print with complementary and contrasting colours. Emphatic central alignment. Paint wash stamped with india rubber on to poster paper.

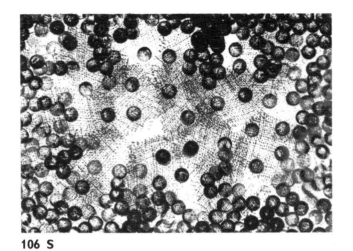

106 S

107 S

108 B 12

50

108: Made from two stamps cut from foam plastic and printed with diagonals running in different directions. Poster paint on drawing paper. 12x16 inches.

109: This print shows various differentiated shapes. Stamp cut from linoleum, and pattern hammered on; print stain on Ingres paper.

109 S

112 B 16

110 B 11

111 B 11

113 B 15

This section is devoted to stick printing, a method which brings out patterns in contrasting black and white. The underplate, which is cut from a piece of linoleum with a knife or linocutting tool, is glued on to a supporting block, preferably a piece of strong plywood. The paint is applied with a lino roller. When making the print you must hammer the stick vigorously. The supporting block must not be too hard, and we recommend setting several layers of newspaper underneath it. The designing is best undertaken with a fresh-cut potato stamp and then applied to the linoleum with draughtsman-like precision. The printing sticks need to be cut with the greatest care; when set side by side they must fit exactly, so that no individual stick is recognisable when the stamping process is repeated.

110, 111: Prints made with one rectangular and two triangular sticks.

112, 113: Individual impressions by the printing sticks used in 114, 115. 6x6 inches.

114 B 15

115 B 16

116 B 14

117 B 14

118 B 14

54

The Rolled Print

To make a rolled print one needs merely a rubber roller, such as is used in lino prints, with print stain, a glass plate and a few minor accessories. The process is simple. A few drops of print stain are dripped on to a glass plate and distributed by repeatedly rolling in all directions with the roller, until both it and the plate are equally stained. All kinds of print stain and multipurpose paint may be used, but the lacquer soluble in water is the most suitable. Oil and turpentine paints take longer to dry; cleaning the tools afterwards is also more bothersome because the respective solvents must be used.

The roller which has been carefully coated with paint is rolled across a sheet of paper. A band of colour results, reflecting the track of the roller in its harmoniously fading grey shades. Such a steady and gradual loss of colour, which results here merely from this rolling process, might well be quite difficult to obtain by using a painter's materials. The mere course of the roller's track is actually of artistic interest, and a wealth of exercises and surface lay-outs can be carried out with it. Before proceeding to surface treatments of this kind we shall show by a series of examples how the track of the roller itself can be varied.

116-134: Surface patterns made by the roller track.

The prints illustrated here are reproduced in original size and show in each case the first three turns of the roller.

116: Single run by the roller.

117, 118: Runs showing the gradual loss of colour. Before the actual print is made the inked roller is turned over section by section on the paper, so that lighter streaks occur over the whole width of the roller itself; these are reproduced on the print, each in its separate space. Narrower streaks occur if in the preparatory stage one merely sets the roller down for a moment without turning it.

119 B 14

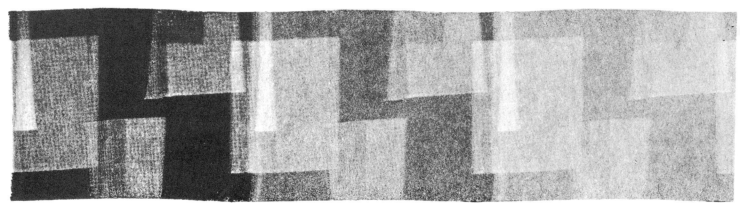

120 B 14

119, 120: Before making this print, guide each section of the roller on its first revolution over a narrow strip of pasteboard, so that bright rectangular areas appear all over the roller. This treatment is especially rewarding wherever brighter areas cut across one another, or overlap on to the next space.

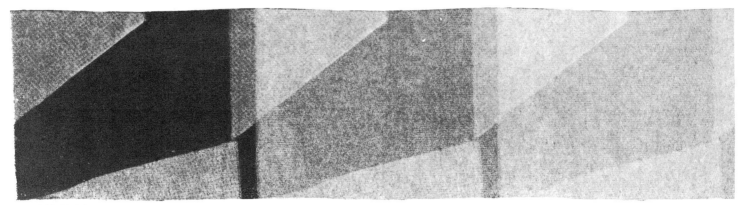

121 B 14

122 B 14

The rough structure of the pasteboard strips imprints itself clearly in the light areas.

121, 122: Effects of the roller's track caused by previously pressing the roller diagonally across a pasteboard strip. A marked stereoscopic effect in 122.

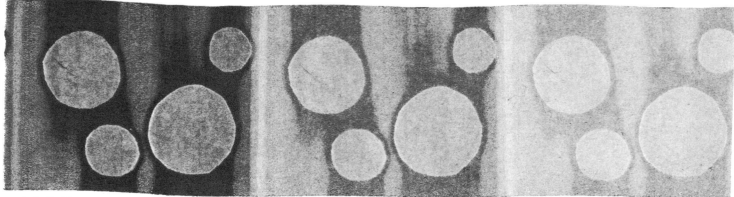

123 B 15

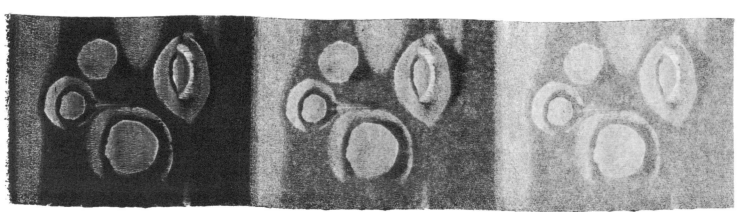

124 B 15

123: The freshly inked roller was turned over four pasteboard discs in its first revolution. At the edges of the discs, and on those parts which were not in contact with the base, the stain has remained in full, so that when the print is taken light and dark surfaces show up outside the circular areas.

124: A print made in the same way, but here in addition smaller discs are laid concentrically on to the larger ones. The roller slipped aside in passing over the discs, so that displaced but very effective plastic shapes emerge.

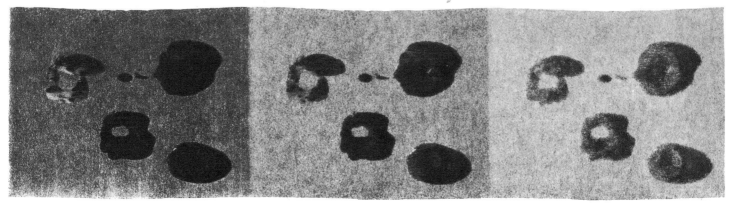

125 G 15

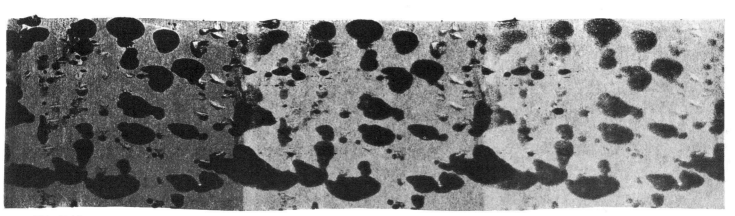

126 G 15

125, 126: Whereas, in the examples so far, stain was partly taken up again from the roller before the print was made, here additional drops of paint have been applied with the brush on to the stained roller. These paint drops, which were squeezed out flat by the first turn of the roller, are reproduced in similar shape and almost similar strength of colour; the surface areas, however, grow lighter with every turn of the roller.

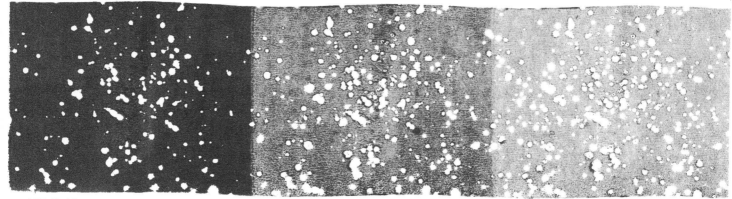

127 B 15

128 T

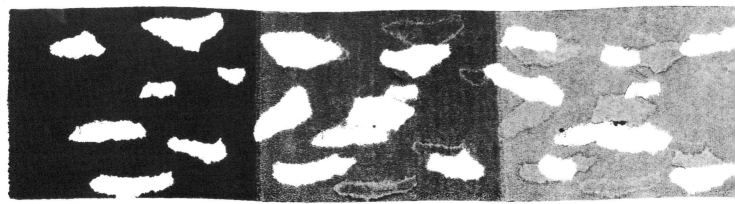

129 B 15

60

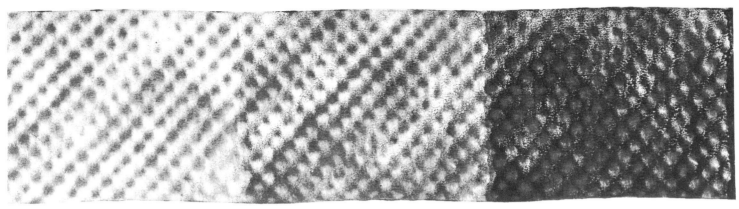

130 G 15

131 T

127-129: Breaking up the roller's track by using transfers. Salt (127) and scraps of cut-out and torn-off paper (128, 129) are scattered on to the surface and rolled in, the patches of the paper which were thus covered remaining white. Tiny grains of salt and scraps of paper remain sticking to the roller in places, and are carried on into the next space, where they leave the impressions of their outlines. In each successive area the shapes grow richer. In this kind of transfer printing the roller must be thoroughly cleaned before each new application of paint.

130, 131: Effects produced with the help of a transfer placed underneath. A sisal fabric, laid under thin paper, prints off in the roller's track with an almost plastic effect.

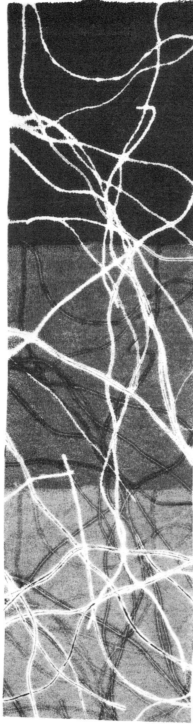

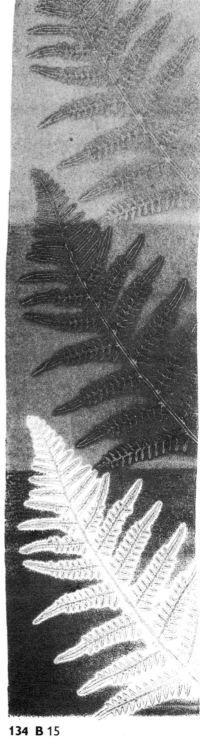

132 G 15

133 G 15

134 B 15

Scraps of cardboard laid underneath the paper surface yield shapes with a soft outline, adding a picturesque effect to the print's character.

132-134: Examples of transfer printing with various materials (material prints).

132: The paint-covered roller is here first of all rolled over a fern leaf in exactly one revolution, so that the fern leaf's shape has imprinted itself on the roller; when the print is made this impression is then reproduced as a negative shape in each space.

133: Threads of a spliced sisal rope are laid on to the base and rolled in. In the final space especially, a lifelike rhythmic line is produced by the imprint of the pattern which had been transferred on to the roller in the previous spaces.

134: A fern leaf which the roller passed over in the first space has been transferred on to the roller as a negative shape, and then been printed off in the remaining spaces.

135-151: Surface patterns made by the roller's track.

135, 136: Lay-outs produced by single runs of the roller in different directions.

137: Graded shades of grey with partial overlapping along short roller tracks.

138: Figuration. Printed with one broad and one narrow roller.

139: Rectangular shapes rolled on in one single direction only. White poster paint on photographic contact paper.

135 B 14

136 B 14

137 B 14

138 S

139 S

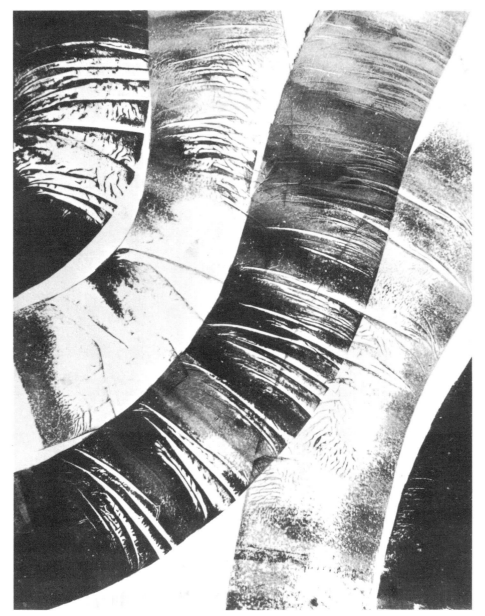

140 S

141 S

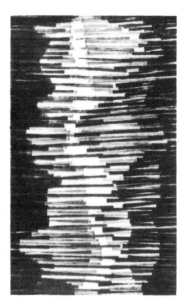

142 S

140: Roller print on thin tissue paper. Example of a print whose character is strongly determined by materials and tools used. The print stain has been applied here with a broad gelatine roller. No clearly defined areas showing each separate revolution of the roller are visible in the track, which gradually grows lighter in colour without any clear break. Under the roller's pressure the thin paper has moved into delicate little creases, and shapes result recalling vegetable growths. 16x24 inches.

If the roller is tilted in its path, or pushed sideways, or turned, intractable impressions result.

141, 143-155: The surface is broken up by a tilted roller into simple, clearly constructed sets of images; untouched areas of the surface play a real part as negative shapes.

142: Gradual loss of colour, with strong surface and linear effects produced by striking with the roller.

143 S

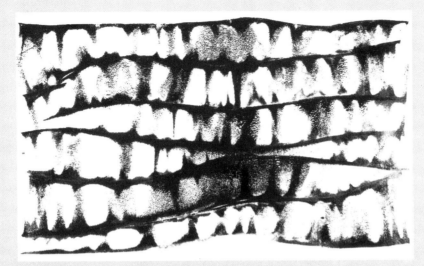

144 S

145 S

146 S   147 S   148 S

The roller print is further enriched if we use the transfer print as made in the single runs already described. Shapes laid under the surface show up, when rolled, as dark patches with soft outlines. Sharply outlined grey patches result when the roller is put over paper transfers laid on the base.

146, 148: Effect made with transfers laid underneath. A thread stuck on to cartridge paper, and a cardboard strip with letters of the alphabet stuck on it, are moved about, twisted and rolled.

147: Print made with the help of a torn cut-out stencil.

149: The surface is broken up with underset transfers (as described for a single run in 131) Balanced arrangements of dark and light patches caused by rolling in opposite directions, and by applying the roller at various spots.

150, 151: Examples of very mature roller prints, freely composed.

150 S

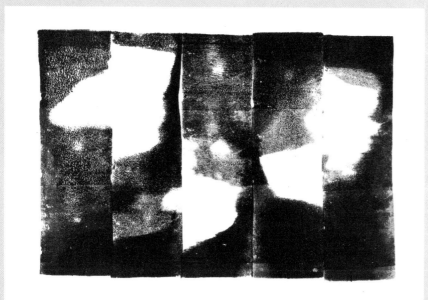

149 T

151 S

152

153 B

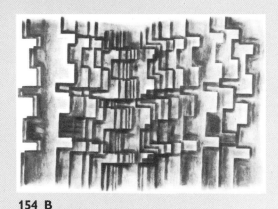

154 B

The Wiping Method

We now proceed to the shading-off effects produced by rubbing away graphite (black lead) from the surface. For this we need ground graphite; if this is not available commercially it can be obtained by scraping a graphite rod, a pencil if necessary. The wiping is done directly with the fingers; for larger areas a paper handkerchief serves well.

Black lead which is freely applied yields gently merging shapes; sharply outlined grey surfaces can be achieved with the help of cut-out paper shapes.

The simplest transfer is a sheet of paper whose edge has been wiped across the base surface; its grey area is darkest on the firm edge (152). In the examples in this section, which have all been produced with the accessories mentioned, it becomes increasingly clear how limited objectives lead to satisfying compositions. Thus 153-163 resulted from a single transfer.

For 153 and 155 the paper sheet was wiped across a smooth cut edge. The looser outline of the torn shape (156) yields a more lively effect than the straight edge. For 154 and 157 transfers were used which had previously been cut out from rectangular and semi-circular surfaces. In 154 the transfer has been pushed to one side, in 157 pushed away, turned over and twisted. The very solid-looking right angles of 158 were produced by wiping with only one corner of a transfer.

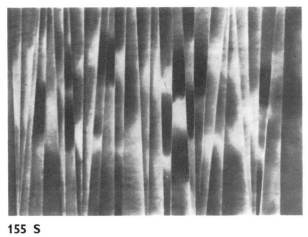

155 S

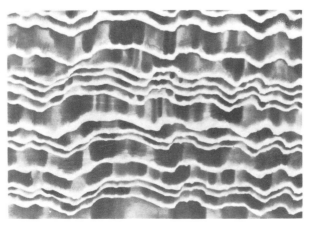

156 S

157 S

158 S

73

159 S

160 S

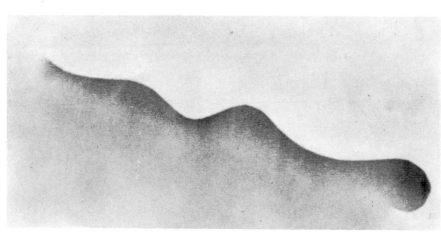

161 S

162 S

159: The lively outline of the torn transfer, and the use of coarsegrained graphite firmly wiped across in opposite directions, give the work a dynamic character.

160: Movement and counter-movement. Fan-shaped arrangement of streaks made by wiping. 12x16 inches.

162: Reflections and the illusion of space. Produced with the help of a thin strip transfer torn along one side which was moved, turned over and twisted. 12x16 inches.

163: For this effect the right angle was used to make the pattern. Illusion of space and depth. Wiped across the corner edges of a large box. 16x24 inches.

163 S

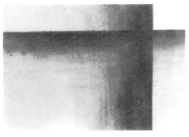

164 S

165 S

166 S

164-166: Surface effects with intersecting grey areas, shown here in contrasting verticals and horizontals. Wiped across the cut edges of a sheet of paper.

167: Landscape, with the illusion of space. Black lead wiped across the edges of a sheet of paper; the sheet itself folded again, and the edges of the folds gently wiped. 16x16 inches.

168: Effect produced by a pointed shape directed towards the centre, with much overpaling and interpenetration. 16x24 inches.

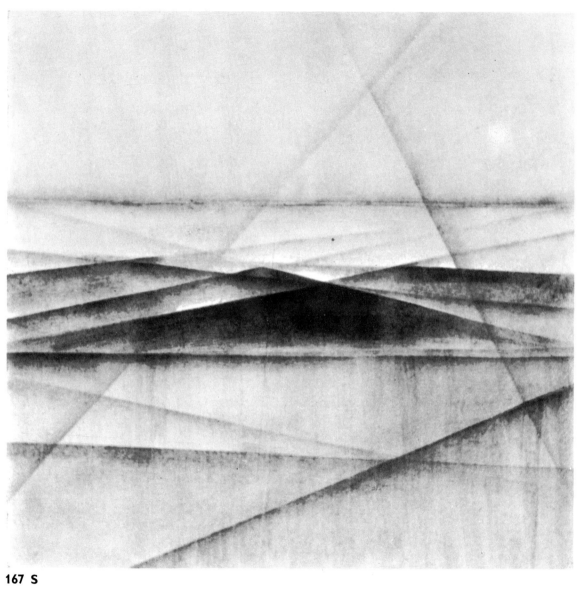

167 S

168 S

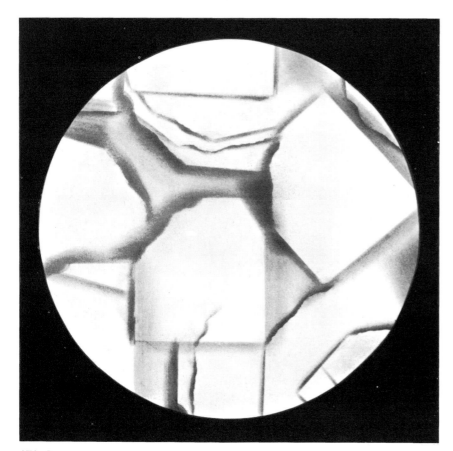

170 S

171 S

Positive and negative transfers are opposite in nature and in effect, as shown in 169 and 172. Black lead is wiped off from a square piece of cartridge paper. The square itself is untouched and appears as a light area on the dark background. A transfer of this kind, which is wiped across from all sides, we call a positive shape. The negative shape is a cut-out. The shape intended is cut from a sheet of paper, or torn out as in 172. Black lead is wiped across it towards the centre, and the shape revealed is a firmly outlined grey area showing the darkest black at the edges. The contrary nature of the effects produced is clearly shown by comparing examples 170 and 173, which were similarly thought out and constructed. For the examples on this double sheet only one transfer was used at a time.

172

173 S

174 S

170: Similar shapes scattered and superimposed. There is an illusion of layering and spacial depth. Rectangular piece of cartridge paper with one corner torn off as the positive transfer. Contrast between cut and torn edges in the basic shape.

171: Square shapes have been scattered, with overlapping in a set direction. Positive transfer.

173: Equal-sized squares have been superimposed with an emphasis towards the centre and with interpenetrating shapes. Cut negative transfer.

174: Similar shapes scattered in a generally central direction and intersecting. Torn negative transfer.

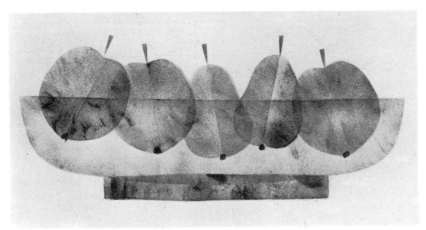

175 **B** 14

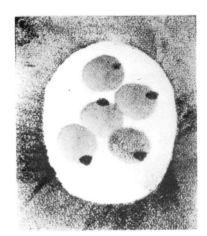

176 **G** 9

177 **B** 15

178 **G** 15

Fruit bowl and insect. Examples for object studies. Even when representing figures, one should limit oneself to few shapes, and these the simplest possible. The shapes are best cut out with scissors along a fold. In this simple process the negative shape is moreover the easiest to produce.

179 **B** 14

180 **G** 15

The construction of the picture with the negative transfer is not absolutely simple, as the transfer hides the base. But both negative and positive forms are made simultaneously when one cuts along the fold, so that the separate shapes can be arranged with the positive, before the negative is applied and its shape wiped clear.

181 S

181: Blossom. A differentiated creation wiped with only two negative transfers. 12x16 inches.

182: This design reminds us of the art of the Far East. Composed with round negative transfers of four sizes. Scattered in a generally upright direction with intersecting shapes. The grey tones diminish harmoniously and shade off delicately in the separate shapes.

84

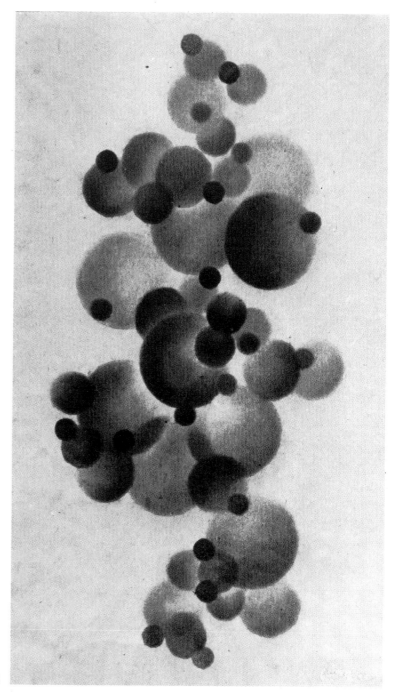

182 S

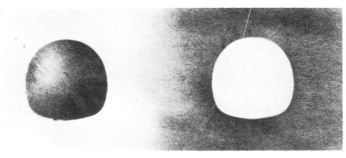

183

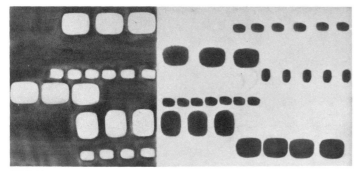

184 S

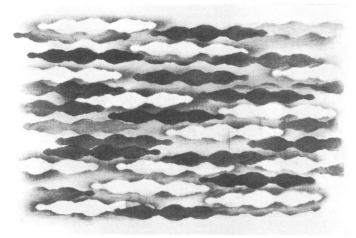

185 S

So far we have been applying the positive and negative transfers separately. 183-199 show work in which both are used together. The alternate interplay of positive and negative is characteristic of these lay-outs. In this series of illustrations this alternation rises from simple juxtaposition of the shapes to a climax with multiple overlaying and interpenetration from opposite sides (194). On analysis—and this may well be left to the student after the detailed descriptions of earlier pieces of work—it becomes increasingly evident that even compositions which appear differentiated, like 193 and 194, are in fact built up from only a few basic shapes.

186 S

187 S

188 S

189 S

190 S

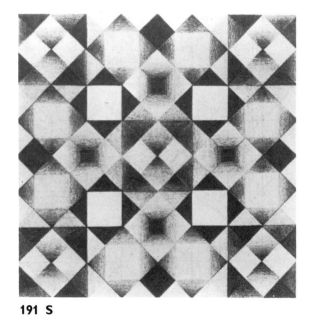

191 S

192 B

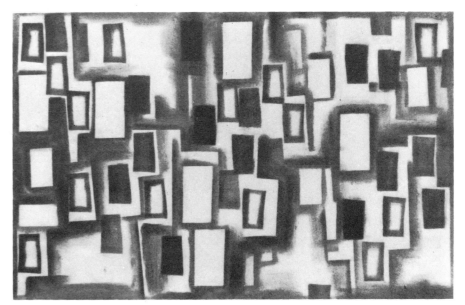

193 S

194 S

195 S

196 B 14

197 S

198 S

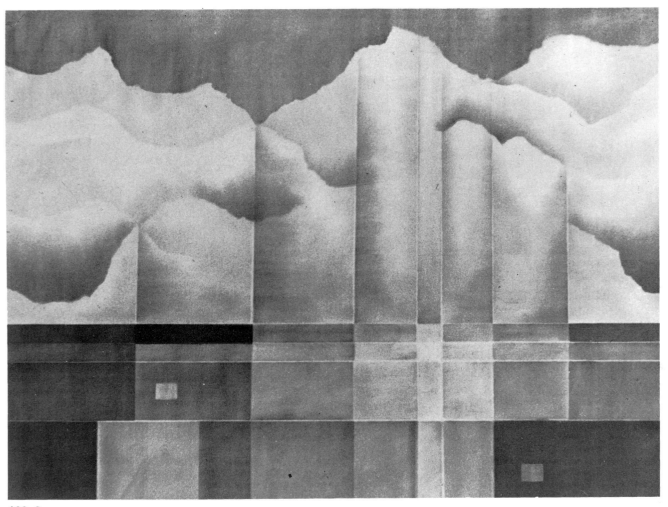

199 S

Surface lay-out on set theme, wiped with positive and negative transfers. 16x24 inches.

200 S 201 S 202 S 203 S

The Spraying Method

The spraying method, using both positive and negative transfers, yielded surface lay-outs in shades of grey with clearly outlined shapes which penetrate and overlay one another.

The paint is sprayed on with a small fixative tube or, by a still simpler process, dusted on through a screen with a toothbrush. All paints soluble in water and applied very thinly are suitable.

200: Freely sprayed paint yielded gently merging shapes.

201-203: Lay-outs built up from the centre with the help from time to time of six cut-out and torn-out positive transfers. Method: the smallest shape—round disc, square, circle—is laid on to the centre of the sheet and sprayed. The sheet receives a light grey shading, the covered surface remaining white. The same process is repeated five times, the next biggest transfer being laid on in turn and sprayed.

When using the spraying method one should start from quite strictly limited exercises, with at first only one constructive element, and using only one size if possible. Countless new shapes can be obtained by overlaying and interpenetration from opposite sides; their inner cohesion is realised only if they are linked by equal basic shapes. Those effects which satisfy most by their simplicity are, in this case too, also the most formally convincing. Thus 204, 206, and 207 are all made from the same-sized constructive element, and 205 from one such unit used in three sizes.

204 S

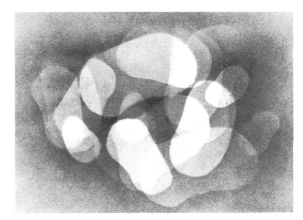

205 S

206 S

207 S

204: Effect produced by using an additional element—a circular disc — as a positive, which remained unmoved to the end; a cut-out stencil of equal size was also used, the dark circular areas being sprayed through it.

206: Here the subdivision of the surface area was clearly planned beforehand. In the top row there are six, in the middle and lower rows five, squares of equal size; when set out they are orientated towards the centre and sprayed in three stages, the transfers being pushed slightly out of position each time.

207: Surface divided up by means of a large square transfer split diagonally; after each spraying every part in turn was slightly displaced, the bottom left-hand corner being the pivot.

208 S

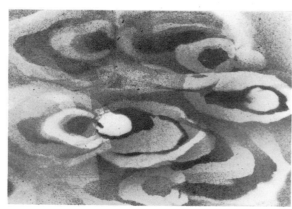

209 S

210 S

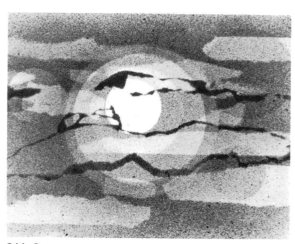

211 S

Examples for lay-outs made by various processes with the help of torn or cut transfers.

208: The triangle as a constructive element; grey shading off without the surfaces intersecting. Triangular transfers were laid on to the base surface and withdrawn one after the other during the spraying. 12x16 inches.

209: Torn transfers moved several times during spraying and folded over at the sides.

210, 211: Combination of torn and cut transfers. 12x16 inches.

212: This lay-out gives a strong effect of space, with firmly outlined grey areas gently swinging away in opposite

94

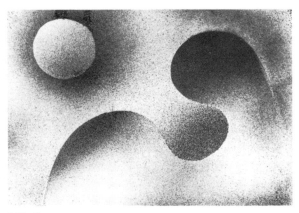

212 S

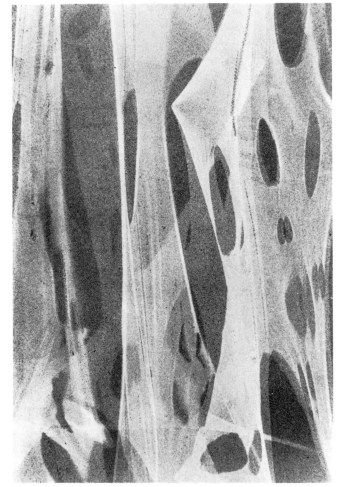

213 S

214 S

directions. We used as transfers a circular disc and both parts of a sheet of paper which had been cut up following closely the direction of the lines.

213: The shapes have pointed corners, and invest the work with a crystalline character. Sprayed with the help of a cover transfer. 8x12 inches.

214: Sprayed work for which nylon stockings stretched across a frame served as the transfers.

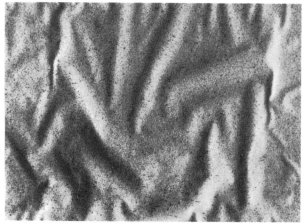

215 S

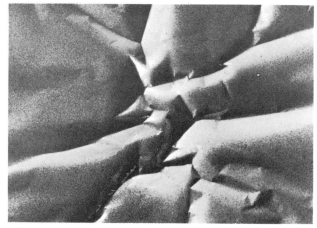

216 S

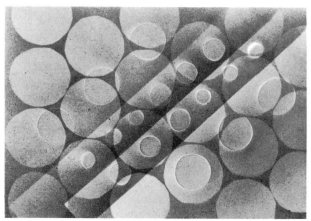

217 S

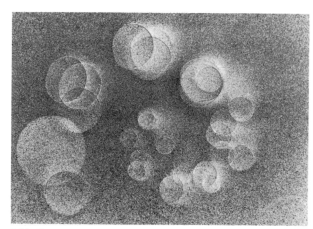

218 S

If corrugated, folded or crumpled papers are hung up vertically and sprayed diagonally from above, they yield effective patterns looking like relief work. A mist of paint settles on the projecting parts, while the areas lying in the spray shadow receive less paint, and remain lighter. Sharp cracks yield firmly outlined areas, and soft folds give gentle transitions. When the surfaces have been smoothed out the firm plastic effect remains. All the examples illustrated here are completely flat paper surfaces.

96

PLATE V, S

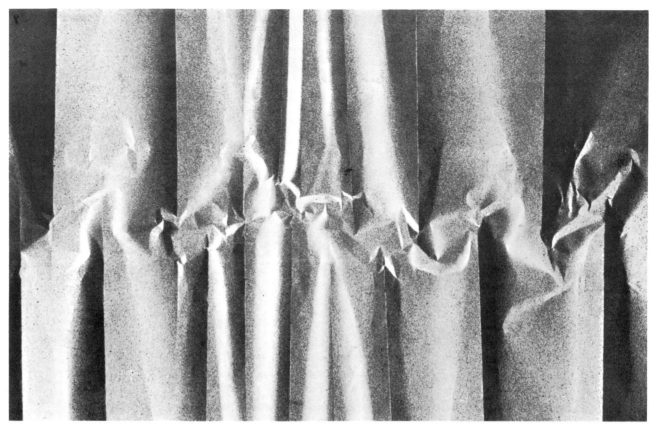

219 S

Before we proceed to stamping through underlaid shapes (217, 218) we must begin with the effects of simple folding, cracking and bending of the surface. Here, too, the exercise should be made perfectly precise by clearly laying down the rules of the game; the nature of the bending, cracking, folding are to be prescribed in detail, and also the number, shape, size and direction of the folds.

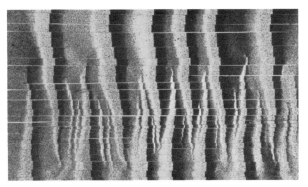

220 S

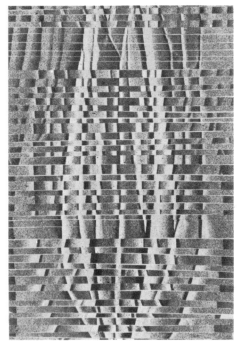

221 S

222 S

223 S

An abundance of surface effects of quite a new kind result from making cracks in the sprayed surface, by moving and exchanging the parts, and finally by using them in a free montage.

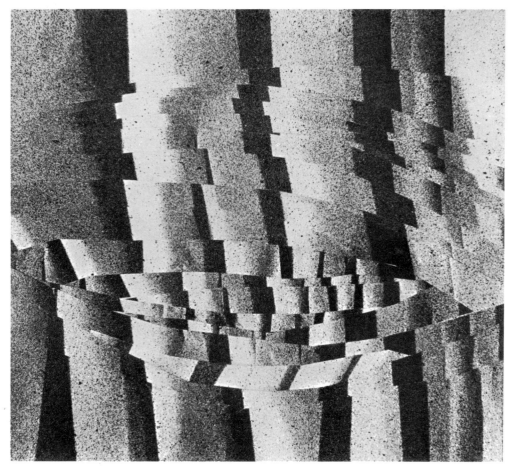

224 S

In 210 and 212 the strips were only displaced; in 221 and 223 they were fitted together to make new designs by displacing, turning and exchanging them.

224 shows a mature surface composition. Above and below the pieces have been moved about, but in the central area several strips have been used to set up a free montage. 12x10 inches.

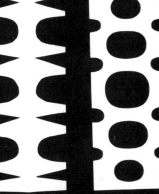

225 G 9   **226 B** 11   **227 B** 12   **228 G** 12   **229 B** 12   **230 G** 12   **231 B** 13

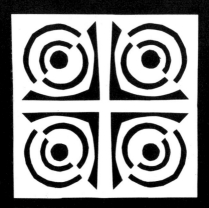
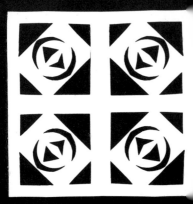

232 B 14   **233 G** 14   **234 B** 14

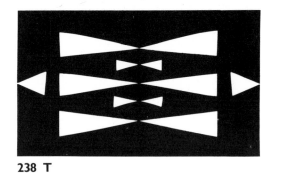

238 T

239 T

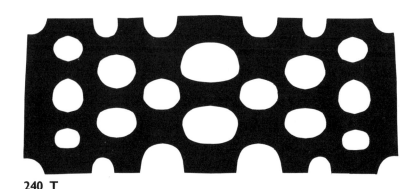

240 T

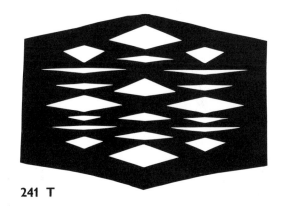

241 T

Breaking up the Surface in Contrasting Black and White and in Shades of Grey: Cutting with Scissors

Cutting with scissors in the simple form of cutting along a fold is easily mastered with creative effect. Symmetrical shapes result like reflections, and with multiple folding arrangements can be repeated.

225-231: Examples from a systematically arranged set of exercises in which a rectangular area was broken up by cutting similar shapes along a single fold; this was done both within the surface area or sometimes on the outside edges.

232-237: Cuts along folds using the square as starting shape. By making a star-shaped fold three times, eight separate thicknesses can be cut at once. Here it is of fundamental importance to choose the simplest shapes.

238-241: Patterns made within the surface by folding similar basic shapes once or several times; the separate shapes can be cut in two or four thicknesses at the same time.

242 T

243 T

244 T

245 T

242-244: Surface broken up by cutting along folds into which are inserted further separate shapes also made by cutting along the folds.

245: Cut shapes are here grouped in an original arrangement along the open edge of a folded sheet of paper.

246: An especially vigorous and rhythmic arrangement of 16 separate shapes made by quadruple folding. When cutting several thicknesses at the same time, be careful not to cut right to the final shape all at once. Such a

102

246 S

procedure would be leaving too much to chance, and with children could result in mere playing about. The actual shaping process will, on the contrary, have to be continuously supervised in its early stages by opening the folded shape after each cut-out, and assessing the arrangement of the newly made shapes. When the exercise is set this continuous control system should also be prescribed, and the folds to be made and the shapes to be cut out should also be precisely determined.

247 T

248 T

249 T

250 G 14

251 T

252 **B** 13

247-258: Studies of objects made by cutting along folds.

251: The basic shape produced by cutting along the folds has here been further developed through separate shapes made by single cuts. This loosens the severe, clean-cut character of the work.

252: Shape made with a razor blade, the lively expression being determined by the nature of the instrument used.

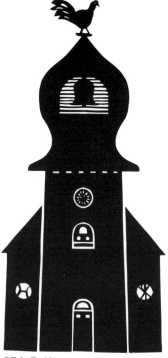

253 B 13

254 B 12

255 B 13

Cut-outs should be made as freely as possible, i.e. without previous marking out. Freshness and immediacy are easily lost if an outline is drawn beforehand. In these towers the shape of the main outline was first freely cut and the interior designs added afterwards. The windows were cut with a lino-cutting tool, knife and razor blade after folding once or twice, that is, in two or four thicknesses.

106

256 J 12

257 S

258 S

A freely made cut-out, here illustrated by 259-263, is technically simpler than when the cutting is along folds; it does, however, present greater formal difficulties, Here, too, it will be better to feel one's way by cutting slowly towards the final shape than to bind oneself down beforehand by a drawn sketch. When working with children, take care that the shapes are cut as large as possible, so that the full length and breadth of the paper is used. 259 is a good example of this strict limitation. The shape of a leaf was to be cut with as little wastage as possible from a rectangular surface, though the original starting shape was to remain recognisable. The whole length and breadth of the original sheet has also been used in the differentiated leaf shape (260).

260, 263: Shapes cut from white paper are stuck on to a black background.

261, 262: Freely cut outlines, the inside cuts made with a lino-cutting tool and razor blade.

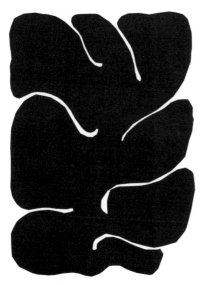

259 B 14

260 T

261 B 11

262 B 13

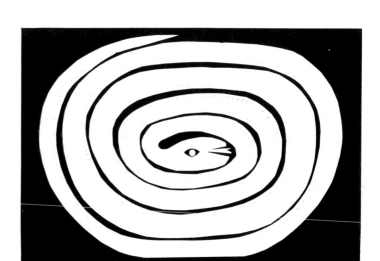

263 T

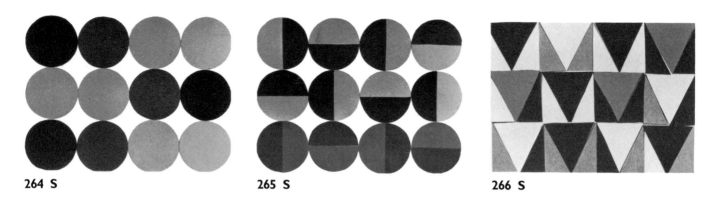

264 S   265 S   266 S

267 S   268 S

Collage

Collage makes it possible to break up a surface by various methods. Here the essential thing is to give starting points, and show how to produce strong rhythmic shapes with the help of black and grey cartridge paper, papers we have coloured ourselves, and industrial papers (printed papers, wrapping papers, illustrated newspapers). Firm cartridge paper is most suitable for a base, and we recommend instant adhesives for sticking, as

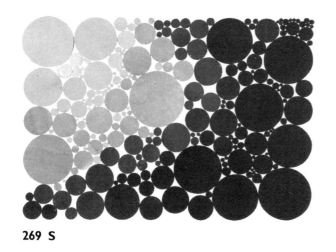

269 S

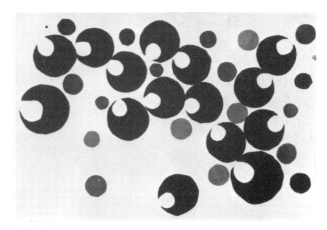

270 S

the surface warps too easily if paste or glue is used. 264-270 show examples for collages with grey and black cartridge paper. In this case the designs were to be executed with only a few geometric shapes in simple creative arrangements in rows or scatters. The rules of the game which formed the basis of the separate exercises can easily be deduced from any of the examples. In patterns of this kind the empty spaces between the stuck-on sections also play their part as negative shapes. In 267 there is a specially rich alternation of equal positive and negative shapes.

In collage work the various pieces should be moved about until a rhythmically interesting solution is found, and not stuck on until then.

271 is an example of another kind of collage, in which the pattern-shaping is effected by layering, and by intersecting shapes. In this piece of work circular discs were cut out from three papers of various shades of grey. The overlaying produces a very strong effect of space. 272 is an example from a series in which collages were stuck together from pieces torn or cut out from a surface previously treated with adhesive paint.

271 S

272 S

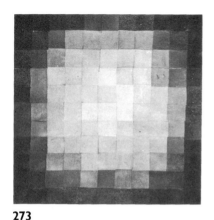

273

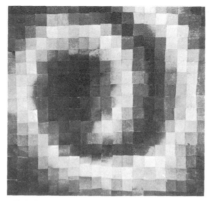

274 S

275 S

Newspapers and illustrated papers provide a rich source of materials for paper collages. 273-286 show what interesting treatments of the surface are made possible in this way. The available supply of plain grey surfaces, grey shades of every tone, composition and design is here so many-sided, even confusing, that a choice must be made with a definite aim in mind. The shapes and the grey tones that are to be used must here be exactly prescribed as a rule of the game.

276 S

It is advisable to begin by sticking on separate square shapes of equal size. In our search to find material we cut out a cardboard stencil the same size as the separate shape in use. This stencil is moved here and there over a picture in an illustrated paper until a spot is found giving the desired effect. This area is marked in pencil and then cut out. The separate shapes are then placed together and can be interchanged amongst themselves until the mosaic-like surface has acquired a balanced rhythm. Only then are the separate pieces stuck on.

277 S

278 S

279 S

273-275: Collages of shaded grey pieces of equal size and shape. Done with a cut-out stencil. Size of the pieces, about one inch square.

279-283: Collages of freely cut- or torn-out shapes of various sizes but of the same tone of grey, and design. 12 x 16 to 16 x 24 inches for 283.

280 S

281 S

282 S

283 S

284 S

285 S

284: Lively contrast between a strict geometrically organised surface (crossword puzzle) and an organic structure (hair structures).

285: Ornamental design from freely cut shapes. 'Blossom'. 12x16 inches.

118

286 S

286: Work on a set subject: 'Landscape'. Contrasted torn-out and cut-out surfaces. 18x12 inches.